KIM K. SANDERS

Hushhhh God is Talking

PROPHETICALLY SPEAKING

HUSHHHH GOD IS TALKING
Prophetically Speaking
ISBN: 978-0-9966222-1-9
Copyright © 2017 Kim K. Sanders

Published By:
Kim K. Sanders International, LLC
P.O. Box 236
Little Rock, AR 72203
www.kimksanders.com

Printed in the United States of America.

All rights reserved. This material is protected by the United States copyright laws. No part of this publication may be reproduced, stored in a retrieval system or transmitted in any form or by any means, electronic, mechanical or photocopying, recording, or otherwise without the prior permission of the publisher.

CONTENTS

ACKNOWLEDGEMENT vii

INTRODUCTION ix

CHAPTER ONE: Prophetic Warnings 1

It's Time To Pray 2

You're Hindering The Process Of What I'm Trying To Do 5

There's A Misconception Here 8

The Church Game 11

Wake Up 16

I Watched A Little Girl 18

Vaginas Don't Talk To Strangers 21

It's Time For Your Deliverance 23

You Cause Her Pain 25

You're Making The Wrong Decisions 27

No Time To Waste 30

What Is This I'm Dealing With? 32

The Devil Is Trying To Suck The Life Out Of You! 36

How Can You Think You're Healthy? 38

CHAPTER TWO: Prophetic Encouragement 41

Be Encouraged 42

I See Your Pain 44

For All You Go Through, There's A Blessing On The Other Side 46

Ghetto Girl To God's Girl 48

I See You, Baby Girl 50

You're Beautiful 51

No Matter What 53

Don't Be Depressed 55

CHAPTER THREE: Reproof 57

Are You Willing To Be Stretched? 58

Let Me Out 61

You Can't Have A Pity Party 63

Love 65

Sight Without Vision 67

The Spirit Of Average 68

Why Are You Broke? 70

Are You Ready To Get Married?... 72

Is He Ready To Be A Pastor? 75

Why Do You Think The Way That You Do?........................... 78

What Is Wrong With You, Man?... 83

CHAPTER FOUR: Prophetic Instructions............................. 85

The Word... 86

Keep It Moving... 88

For Such A Time As This... 92

It's Time To Fly... 94

From Caterpillar To Butterfly 95

Look For The New 97

It's Time To Give 99

Don't Be Distracted 102

It's Time To Get Your Money 104

Go Get Your Money Now!.. 106

Get Ready For Your Husband 108

Don't Try To Explain 111

KIM K. SANDERS

He's A Good Man.. 114
A Couple To Be Admired 116
THE END 118
ABOUT THE AUTHOR 121

ACKNOWLEDGEMENT

To my Lord and Savior Jesus Christ, Thank you for the grace to complete this project in less than 10 days. I am honored that You would choose me to communicate Your heart and articulate the prophetic word of the Lord.

To my wonderful husband Ernest Sanders Jr., who helped to make this book a success, this would not be possible without you. I would like to give a special thanks to my son, Ernest Sanders III. Thank you for your awesome photography and helping me to bring my vision to life.

INTRODUCTION

The composed words in this book are not an echo, but rather the authentic, prophetic utterances from the mouth of God.

The oracles of God are articulated through poetic expression and rhymes, giving prophetic warnings, reproof, encouragement and divine instructions to the Church.

To capture the essence and true voice of the spoken word, I encourage you to read out loud. Some parts are written in first person as God is directly speaking, while other parts are prophetically speaking in third person.

He that has an ear to hear, let him hear what the Spirit of the Lord is saying.

CHAPTER ONE

Prophetic Warnings

It's Time To Pray

It's time to pray like never before
In order to birth forth and receive more.
This is not the time to be passive;
God is getting ready to release the massive.
You must become violent and take it by force;
You've got to be consistent and stay on course.
Consistency is the key to breakthrough prayer;
Until you see manifestations, you must remain there.
Gather your promises and speak them everyday
To avoid interruptions in the Spirit to cause delay.
The effectual fervent prayers of the righteous avail much,
Affecting cities, states, even nations
Many lives you will touch.
It's time for change;
It's time to produce the new.

HUSHHHH GOD IS TALKING

So stay in position so God can use you.
Prayer is the birthing place where things come to pass,
The place to receive power and authority to last.
It will be hard to make it without prayer as a lifestyle.
I suggest you get with God's program;
It will be worth your while.
It's either God's way or the World's;
There is no in between.
You must choose His way
So He can intervene.
In your personal affairs and all things in earth,
He wants you to understand
The value of prayer and its worth.
Prayer is the force that changes all things;
It uncovers strategies and demons behind the scenes.
There are spirits working behind situations
that you can't see
Designed to keep you in the midst of misery.
They're assigned to strategically plot and plan
Against every child, every woman and every man.

They want to keep you ignorant and on the defense,

Always wondering what's going on and in suspense.

It's time to rise up on the offense;

And take your stand,

With a victory mentality, ready to command!

It's time to pray, People of God,

Like never before

So you'll be ready for whoever comes knocking at your door!

You're Hindering The Process Of What I'm Trying To Do

You're hindering the process of what I'm trying to do.

You're allowing everything around to keep distracting you.

These are fatal distractions to your destiny,

Designed to take you out and bring insanity.

To distract means to disturb or trouble greatly in mind.

It also means "to puzzle;" insanity and madness you'll find.

To make complicated, difficult, or confused,

You're allowing yourself to be mentally abused.

So, what do you plan to do? Just lie down and die?

Because the battle that you're in will only intensify.

You haven't been feeding yourself any spiritual food,

Which causes you to be empty, drained, and in this type of mood.

KIM K. SANDERS

You don't have a balance or spiritual covering in your life.

I ordained spiritual authority to protect against this type of strife.

In spite of what you believe, you must be in subjection to authority,

To come against the powers and tactics of the enemy.

You must have integrity in every endeavor,

Or you'll reap what you sow, a principle that works forever.

This world is made of principles and laws that are already set.

When ignored or applied, they cause laws to go into effect.

When you ignore a law,

Things will get worse or things will remain the same.

When you apply a law, you have the power and authority to command things to change.

You've been violating laws for several years,

But you appear to be successful among your peers.

I desire that you experience prosperity My way,

Which requires you to be consistent and focused each day.

HUSHHHH GOD IS TALKING

You must reposition yourself and get things in line.

Those things that I speak to you, you're running out of time.

Everything that's not of Me, it must go;

It's hindering the process of your flow.

You must remove the distractions and people around,

Who are causing you delays and pulling you down.

You must act now; you cannot delay.

There's no time to waste; do it today.

There's a pattern in your life that I desire to break;

It causes these distractions that you allow, accept, and take.

You're a person of influence; I have to deal with you strong and severe.

Take heed to this word with holy, reverential fear.

There are things that I'm trying to get to and through you.

Stop hindering the process of what I'm trying to do!

There's A Misconception Here

There's a misconception and mindset here
that needs correcting,

That will cause crop failure while you're
believing and expecting.

You're looking within the four walls to meet your needs

When God's got more than one way to bring in seeds.

Seed for one person may be harvest for another;

Whatever the case may be, God has enough to cover.

The churches are pimping each other
passing money around,

Scared of the world's money, keeping each other bound.

Stop hustling people to give money to you,

When man is just a vessel for money to come through.

Too lazy to labor, using man to take your place,

Money won't show up until you get on your face.

That means speaking the Word in order for you to see

HUSHHHH GOD IS TALKING

Your words are a force that will produce reality.

But first, you must believe before speaking in
the atmosphere.

Out of an established heart only will open heaven's ear.

Heaven can't participate in illegal affairs on earth;

It needs man's permission through prayer
to give birth.

Man, giving God legal right to interfere

God gave man authority and dominion down here.

Some of you are barren and can't conceive

Because when I try to plant, you reject
and won't receive.

Then you who have been pregnant, but can't
carry full term

Because your seed didn't take root;
you miscarried the sperm.

Others have given birth to seeds that are corrupt.

When I tried to uproot them,
you told Me "Don't interrupt."

Show Me a plant without a root that is surviving,

And I'll show you a man without the

Word that is thriving.

KIM K. SANDERS

The seed of the spirit world is the words you speak;

The seed of the physical world is the money which you seek.

You'll never live above the seeds that you sow;

Your quality of life is determined by the seeds you grow!

The Church Game

Don't get caught up in the church game people play;

All around the World you see it in the church every day.

First, you've got those who just got saved;

They come into the church learning how to behave.

They get a little Word and get a little zeal,

Drawn to dessert instead of getting a full meal.

It's dangerous just enough to destroy a person's life,

Still full of anger, jealousy, envy, pride and strife.

Well, of course, they won't admit it because they're usually in denial;

It shows on their countenance, and their attitudes are foul.

Wow! All that singing, dancing and speaking in tongues!

And be the main ones shouting at the top of your lungs!

Now you say church folks ain't right and say they be trippin',

KIM K. SANDERS

But yet you still be tipping, slipping and dipping.

You talk about the preachers and how they're not right,

But the hypocrite in you is a freak show at night.

Night represents the dark where people can't see

The hidden secrets in your closet that keeps
you from being free.

I'm not necessarily talking about any particular sin;

I'm talking about those things that keep tormenting you
over and over again.

You are the "church folk" that you be talking about;

You need a transformation from the inside out.

Now, don't get me wrong; leaders have the same
problems too,

Hiding behind the pulpit and the Word is what they do.

When I look at some leaders and look at their churches,

I see the blind leading the blind.

No real deliverance, no real understanding of
church structure is what I find.

Wanting to be a Pastor, Bishop, Apostle or a Prophet,

No power, no mantle, just a title; you know
you need to stop it.

HUSHHHH GOD IS TALKING

You call yourself a doctor; a doctor over what?

When you need major surgery, still stuck in your rut.

All your degrees and honorary doctorates
don't mean jack;

It's the authenticity of the anointing and power that you
should really pack.

Why do African Americans feel like they
need that validation?

Because you rarely see that in the race
among the Caucasian.

Joyce Meyer is a prime example of one who
doesn't have a degree,

Changing lives all over the world without
a title or a PHD.

You can't use the excuse you need the title

"Dr." for God to open a door;

What God can do for one, He'll do for
you and even more.

Yes, there are some that have the title and those
that God does ordain

Those who have been proven, paid the price,

Having gone through much labor and pain.

KIM K. SANDERS

I could understand if you were Creflo Dollar,

Fred Price, Bishop Hilliard or Cindy Trimm;

They've earned the title "Dr." but you don't even compare to them

No signs and wonders following, you haven't

labored or paid a real price'

A reproach to the Kingdom, with your broke self, fronting and looking real nice.

Trying to lead the people places that you've never been,

When you have no real authority in these areas in your life to win.

Preaching about the overflow when you're not even full,

Giving a bunch of scriptures and text when you're really full of bull.

Leaders caught up in the game of the church, not knowing who they really are,

Full of yourself with fifty armor bearers; desiring to be a star.

Looking for a hook up; not wearing the real blessing,

Begging the people for money, instead of believing and confessing.

Out of the same mouth you speak the blessing, then speak a curse,

HUSHHHH GOD IS TALKING

Not having the power to change situations when things seem to get worse.

Laying hands on the people when you need healing yourself,

In need of deliverance; always depressed and in bad health.

Operating in the gifts, not bearing the fruits,

WOW! What a shame!

You need the Hand of God laid on you

So you can stop playing the church game.

So if you're going to wear the title,

Be clothed with the mantle and let God appoint;

He's only obligated to support and backup those that He calls and anoints!

Wake Up

You've wasted many days, weeks, months and years.

You've been traumatized, paralyzed and bound by many fears.

In a prolonged state of unconsciousness that's deep,

Waiting to be rescued from your comatose sleep.

Trapped inside this body, your spirit is crying out.

Oh wounded soul, causing mental shock is what brought this about.

You've been infected and poisoned; an injury has taken place.

I see a person unable to respond when

I look at your face.

I see gifts lying dormant, waiting to be stirred.

I see life passing you by, God's plans being deferred.

There's been no peace, no joy, unhappy you are.

Still broke, still lazy, you haven't gone very far.

HUSHHHH GOD IS TALKING

You've allowed things to send you into a cardiac arrest,

All types of emotional damage that has caused you to be depressed.

The cold blows of life have been more than a notion.

Sleepwalking through life like a zombie,

You've just been going through the motions.

You've been inactive, lethargic, living in a trance,

Pressing your way through, hoping to advance.

It's time to wake up, be quickened, arise and shine

To the awareness of life, to the taste of new wine.

Get excited, stirred up, aroused and stimulated!

Be revived, reawakened, be provoked, get motivated!

Stay focused, renew your mind, pay attention and re-educate.

Embrace your future, love yourself; Now, go activate!

I Watched A Little Girl

I watched a little girl grow up, so precious, dear and pure.

Just like all little girls start out until they begin to mature.

She used to play with dolls, like Barbie and Ken.

Now, she's interested in playing with grown men.

She carries a body of a woman that's 29;

But, yet still young and immature in her mind.

She thinks that she's grown, but can't make the right choices,

Listening to deception and all the wrong voices.

Looking for love in all the wrong places,

Living a double life, wearing two faces.

Can't seem to stop, think, and slow down,

Chasing after a joker, looking like a clown.

Mixed up in the head with a mental dysfunction,

HUSHHHH GOD IS TALKING

Steadily ignoring the Holy Ghost's unction.

Take heed to this warning and don't self-destruct;

God gave you a free will that He can't interrupt.

There have been many prophecies spoken over your life,

But they won't come to pass living in disobedience, rebellion, and strife.

No matter how much you lie, pretend and put on a façade,

You've come to a place now where this thing is between you and God.

I will no longer be the police over you 24/7;

It's your responsibility to secure your own place in heaven.

You can't continue to use as an excuse,

"Nobody loves me, so what's the use?"

I've given you love and reached out with much grace,

But, you continue to defile yourself going back to the same old place.

It's a place of no return if you don't change your ways;

It's a place you'll spend in turmoil for the rest of your days.

KIM K. SANDERS

God shall not be mocked; you shall reap what you sow.

Get it right before it's too late, and no
one will even know.

What profits a man to gain the whole world
and still lose his soul?

Stop allowing yourself to stay under the devil's control!

Vaginas Don't Talk To Strangers

Vaginas don't talk to strangers; who have you been talking to?

Your body is God's temple; He dwells inside of you.

We're living in perilous times; we're living in the last days,

Where men will be lovers of pleasures and wicked in all their ways.

Turn away from sin and put away your lust.

Vaginas don't talk to strangers; holiness is a must.

Crucify your flesh and walk in purity;

I've set you apart and called you unto me.

Just in case you think you're gay, who told you that lie?

I bind that unclean spirit and command that spirit to die!

You have a form of Godliness, but, you deny the power thereof;

You continue to defile yourself and run away from my love.

KIM K. SANDERS

Baby, can't you see what the devil's trying to do?
Vaginas don't talk to strangers is what
I keep telling you.
The devil comes to kill, steal and destroy;
He's throwing you around and using you like a toy.
The devil would love to keep you caught up in the mix;
He's full of the same old perverted sex tricks.
Vaginas don't talk to strangers; God wants you to know
You don't have to settle for just any old Joe Blow.
Get washed in the blood, and you don't have to date;
Just pray and ask God to send you your mate.
How will I know if he's the right bait?
Because vaginas don't talk to strangers and
he'll know he has to wait.

It's Time For Your Deliverance

It's time for your deliverance if you want
your life to last.

Some things can only be destroyed by going on a fast.

The enemy has been working hard, time and time again.

To kill, steal, and to destroy, and you keep
letting him win.

Your battle is against spirits that you cannot see

That constantly keep you from walking in the victory.

The reason that you toss and turn throughout the night,

Is the enemy wants to keep you tangled up in a fight.

There are strongholds in your life that need to
be pulled down,

That are holding you in bondage and keeping you
bound.

You walk around with anger, fear, confusion,
torment and pride,

When you know you're deeply wounded;

I see all the hurt inside.

KIM K. SANDERS

When will you let me heal you and take away the pain?

You have nothing to lose but everything to gain.

These words are not to offend you,
but sent to set you free.

I desire that you totally surrender your whole self to Me.

You haven't scratched the surface of who I really am.

You don't understand this shedding
of the blood of the lamb.

I desire that you know Me and that you seek My face;

You must have My word in you in order
to stay in this race.

The race is not given to the swift, but
only to those who last.

In order for Me to heal you, you must
first forget the past.

Don't keep giving in to all of the enemy's tricks;

Being stubborn, which is witchcraft,
will keep you in the mix.

It's time to change your ways and crucify your flesh.

Repent, and I will cleanse you, and you can start afresh.

Don't be ashamed; just make a brand new start.

Come to Me, My child, and let Me heal your heart.

You Cause Her Pain

You cause her pain, a pain that goes deep.
A pain that causes her to continue to weep.
It's a pain that hurts deep inside,
A wound that won't close, that's opened wide.
What do you expect for her to do,
When she continues to keep telling you
The devil is using you to try to take her mind?
But thank God she has discernment and thank God she's not blind.
What has to happen in order for you to see
That you need deliverance and need to be set free?
You need to surrender and tell God yes;
Don't be deceived in thinking that God will bless mess.
So, drop the pride and whatever's holding you back,
Or you'll continue to be an open target for attack.

Stop transferring blame and take a look within.
Stop yielding to the devil and letting him win.
You don't want to pay the price of a fruit called sin,
Doing the same old things over and over again.
So, stop causing her pain and crucify your flesh.
Renew your mind to the Word so God can really bless!

You're Making The Wrong Decisions

You're making the wrong decisions out of
the arm of the flesh,

Decisions that will lead your life into a bigger mess.

I know it's a lot that you don't understand,

But, I can only speak those things to your spirit man.

There's a pattern in your life that I desire to break,

That causes these decisions that you continue to make.

Your spirit man is restless, and you don't have any peace.

You carry a spirit of heaviness and it
continues to increase.

Your mind is being pressured, tossed to and fro.

Demons hunt you down everywhere you go.

When you try to move forward,
you seem to get set back.

Everywhere you turn around there's a spirit of lack.

KIM K. SANDERS

The enemy wants you to think that it
will always be this way.

To keep you in bondage and paralyzed each day.

There's a deception going on to keep
you feeling trapped.

It's a generational curse that has
transferred and attached.

You're dealing with a spirit that you can't even see.

That spirit has been hiding, keeping you from reality.

That spirit wants to entrap you and
pull you deep, deep within,

Holding you prisoner, tormenting
you over and over again.

There's a soul tie here that needs to be broken.

Warning comes before destruction;
take heed because I have spoken.

The road that you are on will lead to
more heartache and pain.

The plan I have for you, there's everything to gain.

Life goes on; it's time for you to be free.

Don't be afraid to let go so you can have total victory.

You've been making wrong decisions;
now it's time to make it right.

I bind the spirit of deception;
open your eyes and see the light.

No Time To Waste

You don't have time to waste; your time is coming near.

Stop allowing the devil to bring torment and fear.

Stop focusing on what you see and speak
the Word for change.

The Word is the key for things to rearrange.

Get busy, get busy and do what you know to do.

Be ready, be ready, for where I'm sending you.

These things are a distraction that you're looking at,

To keep your mind preoccupied with
things like this and that.

I put a strong Word in you; it's like fire
shut up in your bones.

I'm getting ready to feature you and take
you away from home.

Although it doesn't seem like it because
of what you're going through.

HUSHHHH GOD IS TALKING

I had to put you in a container in order
to pour in the new.

I know you get lonely; so put your whole self in Me.

I had to remove the old in your life and all the Pharisees.

The blessing of the Lord is stretching you
out of your comfort zone,

An unfamiliar place that you must walk alone.

People won't be able to hold you down to
who they think you are.

I'm stretching you out and stretching you wide,
so you can go very far!

What Is This I'm Dealing With?

First, you must realize that you're dealing with a spirit.

It's foul, it's cunning, designed to make you fear it.

This spirit will manifest itself in several forms.

It comes to frustrate, harass and take you
through many storms.

Know that it's something you can't handle on your own.

You need the power of God on this spirit to dethrone.

It comes with a mission to destroy,

To rob and strip you of your joy.

It causes chaos, turmoil, and confusion.

It carries disorder and a spirit of delusion.

This spirit is corrupt, twisted, and perverted.

It's wicked with thoughts that are planted and diverted.

The thought patterns of the individual
are often insane.

Though they're highly intelligent and gifted,

HUSHHHH GOD IS TALKING

to think normal is a great stain.

They do strange things that you never would believe,

Not realizing that they hurt you; but in their minds they can't conceive.

They live a life of deception, torment, and fear.

They have the wrong perception of things; they don't see things clear.

Their mind is tossed to and fro with no emotional stability.

They resist and reject the people who have the power to set them free.

They deal with continuous racing and scattered thoughts.

They rarely apologize and they justify their faults.

They'll argue you down and start a debate,

Causing you to fight feelings of bitterness and hate.

They lean towards people, who are weak and passive,

To make themselves feel strong and appear massive.

When threatened or challenged, they go into a rage.

They attack and intimidate you like a lion let out of a cage.

They use manipulation, rebellion, and control.

There's an ugly, evil spirit that rises up
with each episode.

They have their own way of doing things,
pretending to submit.

When they can't have their way, they throw
tantrums and have a fit.

They roam around with sleepless nights with
depression as a weight.

They're strong-willed, full of pride,
but so easy to intimidate.

They have a giving spirit, but yet

self-centered; it's always about them.

Nothing you do is ever enough, even
when it comes through Him.

They're very critical, extremely insecure,
and always on the defense.

They get easily offended and put up a front,
with behavior of false pretense.

They wear two faces: Dr. Jekyll and Mr. Hyde.

They also have a strong, abnormally high sex drive.

This spirit comes through a generational curse.

Each generation it travels, the seed gets worse.

It's called a mental disorder that's usually hereditary.

HUSHHHH GOD IS TALKING

It's a deep rooted spirit that a lot of people carry.

You may have it and you're just not aware.

It hasn't been diagnosed, but all the signs are there.

You may be thinking, "This ain't none of me she talking about."

But deep in your soul, that spirit is hiding and it doesn't want to come out.

Whether you admit it or not, these are facts you can't deny.

The spirit doesn't want you to receive truth, no matter how hard you try.

If you're being affected by this disease, get help because it won't go away

Until you first come out of denial and put the Word in your spirit every day.

I believe there's no manner of sickness and disease that God cannot heal.

It's nothing to be ashamed of in spite of how you may feel.

It's just like any other disease except this one comes for your mind.

Take authority over this strongman; it's the deaf and dumb spirit to bind.

The Devil Is Trying To Suck The Life Out Of You!

The devil is trying to suck the life out of you;

A door has been opened for him to come through.

He's attacking your body; your immune system is weak.

Your body is drained and you're too tired to speak.

He's trying to shut you down, a threat
to his kingdom you are.

Because of what you carry, he can't let you get too far.

New seeds have been planted that you've got to get out.

The sapsuckers are gone; so, he's taking a new route.

If he can get your body, then next is your mind.

You must take care of your temple with

God's original design.

Divine healing is God's original plan.

Rest, vitamins and supplements, our body will demand.

HUSHHHH GOD IS TALKING

Don't compromise the nutrients your
cells and body need;

It's a must in your system in order to proceed.

When the rate of damage exceeds the rate of repair,

Disease can occur and cause the body despair.

To quickly replenish, take some vitamin C;

You also have a vitamin B deficiency.

You must use wisdom and give your body rest;

Your body is God's Temple, and He needs
you at your best.

Stay on the offense by doing your body right;

Your body is not designed to put up this type of fight.

The enemy's mission is to assassinate;

You're one of the ones he despises and hates.

You're a life giver; you have many more
doors to go through.

That's why the devil is trying to suck the life out of you!

KIM K. SANDERS

How Can You Think You're Healthy?

How can you think that you're healthy

And you keep eating the wrong things?

Ham, pork chops, chocolate cake and fried hot chicken wings?

You can't lose weight or be healthy eating these types of foods.

This is a misconception that's setting your patterns and moods.

You must eat to live, not live to eat.

What's the root of the problem that's causing your defeat?

How can you think that you're healthy and you won't exercise?

I say won't because it's a choice that you seem to despise.

We do what we want and sacrifice what we need.

But, when diseases show up, to God we beg and plead.

HUSHHHH GOD IS TALKING

Then you want to act like you're ready and sincere,

Adding to your struggle, discouragement and fear.

Deception says you're too weak to break through;

So, you'd rather remain.

But how can you be too strong to keep bearing the pain?

Well, "I'm just not ready for all of that," is what you say.

But, your body is God's Temple; you'll pay a price either way.

You're just like someone not ready to accept Jesus as their Lord,

Sounding silly and deceived, something you both can't afford.

What are you waiting on to change your mindset?

Cancer? Heart disease? They're waiting in line to take effect.

Sickness ought to be enough to get you motivated.

Seeing what it does to you should be enough to hate it.

You keep playing with this thing and won't renew your mind,

Making excuses, thinking you've got lots of time.

Your time is running short; that's what you can't see.

It's time to discipline your flesh and
develop consistency.

I know you're not offended because
what I'm saying is true.

These are things that you already know you need to do.

It's a reproach to the kingdom to be
depressed, broke or sick.

As the world watches us wondering,
satan's laughing, getting his kick.

Who's in better shape, the world or you?

Now the question remains, what are you going to do?

Follow My commandments and natural
laws; give ear to what you hear.

Then none of these diseases will come on you

That are chasing you far and near.

Renew your mind to new seeds;
plant and allow them to grow.

You'll produce results that are pleasing
in your life it will show!

CHAPTER TWO

Prophetic Encouragement

Be Encouraged

Be encouraged Child of God; help is on the way.

Sometimes you must encourage yourself;
let Me tell you what to say.

"I refuse to sit here and be depressed and let
the devil win.

I must guard my heart with the Word,
so the enemy cannot get in.

The devil is roaming to and fro seeking
whom he may devour.

But greater is He that is in me, the Word
that's full of power."

The love of God is the greatest commandment
that you will ever have.

I guarantee if you'll walk in that love,
you will have the last laugh.

Come out of your flesh. Walk in the spirit.

I'm calling you to a higher place.

Keep pressing to Me behind the veil and here,

HUSHHHH GOD IS TALKING

I'll show you My face.

It doesn't matter what's going on around you;
look to the third realm.

Trust in Me with your whole heart and

I will take care of them.

"Vengeance is mine," saith the Lord;
don't worry about what's been done.

Hold your head up high and know
that the battle's been won.

It doesn't matter what people think;
they may never understand you.

But I'm holding you accountable for what you say,
think, or do.

So, have a deaf ear to what you hear and a
blind eye to what you see.

Stop wasting your time explaining yourself
and stay focused on Me!

I See Your Pain

I see your pain, deep down in your heart.

I've been there all along, right from the start.

You've cried at night and hurt through the day.

You smile at people because you really can't say.

Sometimes you wish people could see what you really go through.

Sometimes it's so bad, you just don't know what to do.

The devil's tried to tell you, "You're going to lose your mind."

You've tried to escape the pain, but the pressure's too much, you find.

"Lord, I don't know how much more of this I can take."

This has been your cry when you lay and when you wake.

You ask yourself, "Will I ever feel real love?"

That love that you desire only comes from above.

I'm here, My child to dry away all your tears.

HUSHHHH GOD IS TALKING

I also desire to take away all your fears.

I want you to know that I love you more
than you can conceive.

That's why I sent My Son for you,
so that you could receive.

I know you've been through a lot,
that words cannot explain.

Open up and let Me in to take away your pain.

Healing, healing, healing, healing is what I do.

I'm healing your mind. I'm healing your soul.
I'm healing all of you.

Yes, you will love again and it will start
by first loving Me.

Then I will teach you how to love yourself.

Which is something you need to see.

This is your season for deliverance,
your season to be free.

Don't look back. Move forward and walk in victory.

For All You Go Through, There's A Blessing On The Other Side

For all you go through, there's a blessing on the other side.

Only God knows how hard you've really tried.

"If only they could see and know my heart," you've said.

No one knows the hurt and the many tears you've shed.

You're in the promised land, but you still have to fight.

Pull out your supernatural weapons and use them with all your might.

You're aware there's been a shift in the spirit and the season has changed.

Keep pressing for the manifestations while things are being rearranged.

You've been given instructions in the natural.

And, you know what you have to do.

Line upon line, precept upon precept is how you must walk this through.

HUSHHHH GOD IS TALKING

Walk in the Spirit My child; the enemy
can't touch you here.

Use the name and the blood, which is
satan's greatest fear.

Consecrate yourself before Me and
I'll speak to you from above.

Make sure you keep yourself saturated in My love.

The vision shall speak and it shall not lie.

It shall be carried out; it shall live and not die.

I've graced those to help you. I'll put
monies in their hand.

They'll have supernatural testimonies
of increase, blessings and land.

So be encouraged child of God, for all you go through.

Know that there's a supernatural
blessing coming to you!

Ghetto Girl To God's Girl

Ghetto girl, ghetto girl, arise and shine.

I'm changing your name; I'm changing your mind.

You won't be the same when I get through with you.

I'm making you over; I'm making you new.

I'm taking away the pain and I'm taking away the drama.

You're more than just a daddy's baby's mama.

You're God's girl; He wants you to know.

You're not a bish.

And, you're not a hoe.

I'm bringing you up and I'm bringing you out.

You don't have to wonder and you don't have to doubt

So, stop crying and dry your tears.

Let me take away all your fears.

Trust in me and not sugar daddy.

Stop giving up your precious catty.

HUSHHHH GOD IS TALKING

I can take care of your every need.
You don't have to beg and you don't have to plead.
I know it gets hard and sometimes rough.
I will always be with you when times get tough.
No need to worry; I'll teach you how to pray.
I'll teach you how to use My Word so
Boo don't have to stay.
So, tell Boo he "gots to go,"
Cause the ghetto girl ain't shackin' no mo'.
Trust in the Lord with all your heart.
And, He will give you a brand new start.
Ghetto girl, ghetto girl, I'm changing your name.
You're God's girl now and you'll never be the same.

I See You, Baby Girl

I see you, baby girl and all that you go through.

You're destined for purpose; I know the plans I have for you.

I want you to know who I made you to be.

I only make originals; you're not a carbon copy.

When you look into the mirror, who do you see?

I created you in My image, so begin to see Me.

Don't try to be like others and pattern after them.

Follow the Holy Spirit and pattern after Him.

This ain't no competition; I didn't make you to compete.

When I designed you before your mother's womb,

You were already complete.

You're more valuable to Me than any diamond, jasper or pearl.

So, hold your head up high! I see you, baby girl!

You're Beautiful

You're beautiful My child, in your own very way.

Don't worry and listen to what others may say.

Your beauty shines from the inside out.

It shows through your countenance without a doubt.

People are jealous of you, which is such a shame.

But, it's not your problem, so, don't take the blame.

God is raising you up for such a time as this.

So hold your head up high; opportunities are in your midst.

Doors of favor are opening unto you,

Doors that you can't be afraid to walk through.

Separate yourself and be careful what you share.

Many won't rejoice with you, but favor ain't fair.

Don't give in to the game that haters play.

Continue to increase yourself and let God have His way.

Don't ever apologize for what God's doing in your life.

KIM K. SANDERS

There are always people full of jealousy, envy and strife.

This is only the beginning of what God's getting ready to do.

So get yourself positioned for Him to feature you!

No Matter What

No matter what you do,
I'll always love you.
No matter where you stay,
I'll love you every day.
No matter where you are,
I'll love you from afar.
No matter what you feel,
My love for you is real.
No matter what you fear,
I'll always be near.
No matter what's been said,
Don't resurrect the dead.
No matter what's been done,
Enjoy life NOW and have fun!
No matter what life brings,

KIM K. SANDERS

Always follow your dreams.
No matter what, it will always be
You and me!

Don't Be Depressed

Don't be depressed; there's nothing to gain,

Except frustration, anxiety, misery, and pain.

Don't be tricked and fall into the devil's hand.

To keep you held captive in your mind is his plan.

You are not confused; you have a sound mind.

You have much power over the enemy, in the Word you'll find.

Stop allowing negative thoughts to torment you night and day.

Make up in your mind, this game you won't allow the enemy to play.

It's like a see-saw, sometimes up and sometimes down.

Designed to take your body straight to the ground.

What must one do to escape the trap that's been set?

Wisdom is the principal thing, and discernment you need to get.

Realize you are in a war whether you want to be or not.

KIM K. SANDERS

So, you might as well learn to use your weapons

Because you'll be needing them a lot.

Satan is already defeated; he's the father of lies.

Full of tactics, gimmicks, games and tricks,
all of which I despise.

But that's what he does; he's good at his profession.

So, what do you expect?

But the greater one lives in you,
so don't let him take effect.

Aren't you tired of your mind running to and fro?

You don't have any peace.

The main reason Jesus died,
so that you could be released.

It's up to you to loose yourself and
be free of the enemy's hold.

The Word says, "If the thief be found,
he shall restore sevenfold."

Be free, child of God. Don't be depressed;
make the enemy pay.

Go get your stuff that belongs to you and
let nothing get in your way.

CHAPTER THREE

REPROOF

Are You Willing To Be Stretched?

Will you let God stretch you like a rubber band?

Come out of you normal position of comfort to expand.

Let Him lengthen, enlarge and stretch you wide.

But it starts by allowing Him to go deep inside.

People are ready to see something different and new.

God is now requiring even more from you.

What worked in the past is not working anymore.

You can't use the same strategies and
patterns from before.

God wants to release a real mantle, a measure of rule,

As you submit yourself to the Holy Spirit's school.

In order to be stretched, there must be great tension

With intense exertion to develop and to strengthen.

God knows the compressive force and
pressure it will take

To produce Generals, true sons and
daughters only He can make.

HUSHHHH GOD IS TALKING

How must one prepare himself for that
wonder working power?

The outpouring of His Spirit in this next
season and final hour?

Your consecration before the Lord,
with prayer and fasting is a must,

Eliminating all sin and every type of hidden lust,

The lust of the flesh, the lust of the eyes
and the pride of life,

Exposing wrong motives, getting rid
of all confusion and strife.

Being submitted to authority,
being able to divinely connect

To God ordained relationships, for the
right deposits to take effect.

You can try to get it somewhere else
but it won't have the same potency.

Only certain people are anointed to
give you authenticity.

Not everyone's ministry produces the same fruit;

Every seed manifested can be traced backed to a root.

So don't be deceived; God shall not be mocked.

Get in the right position for His power to be unlocked.

KIM K. SANDERS

A place of obedience, discipline and consistency,

With a heart of giving, love and transparency.

So, let God stretch you in the bow so

He can pull the arrow.

Hitting bulls-eye in that strategic atmosphere, ready to face every Pharaoh.

He's launching you forward, further and fast.

With a solid foundation so you can last!

Let Me Out

Let me out! Let me out! I'm trapped inside,

Waiting to burst loose, to burst open wide.

Oh, there's a lot of agony, hurt and pain in here,

Rejection and torment coupled with fear.

I want to pursue my goals, but I've been too afraid

To release the hidden parts of me, the real me God made.

I've been told that I'd never be nothing and all that I can't do,

Looking in the mirror, seeing myself through other people's view.

I have a deep desire to be all that I can be.

But, it somehow got buried in the company of misery.

Being trapped in this cobweb has allowed me to see

All the setbacks, disappointments, and my insecurity.

Thinking less of myself and my ability to perform

Made me think I'm just ordinary and being average is the norm.

KIM K. SANDERS

Apathy caught a hold of me, a place of no return.

At least that's what I thought until my
heart began to burn,

Only to realize that deception has taken place.

But, will I live in denial or is this something

I'm willing to face?

Will I confront my issues, my weaknesses and be real?

Will I allow the transformation and the
power of God to heal?

I feel like I'm trapped in a mannequin, hard,
lifeless, and dead.

Can't you hear me screaming or is this
all just in my head?

How bad do you really want it? Are you
willing to break through

All the hindrances, distractions
and strongholds pulling you?

You can come out, but the ball is in your court.

This is your life and destiny that you're
almost about to abort.

Let yourself out and grab hold of My hand.

Accept Me first, accept yourself and
then follow my plan.

You Can't Have A Pity Party

You can't afford to have a pity party; get up from there!
Trying to feel sorry for yourself, don't you even dare!

What is the matter with you? You know

God's been good.

Always providing for you, just like He said He would

Don't be like the Israelites wandering for 40 years.

Going around the same ole mountain
afraid to face their fears

Now, who do you know wants to come to a
party of this kind?

Misery loves company, that's the type you'll find.

Stop talking about your problems to everyone who
comes around,

Imparting your drama, pulling people down!

Stop all this madness and put vision before your face.

Time is precious; moments you don't have to waste.

Now, what have you allowed to get on the inside

KIM K. SANDERS

That's causing this door to be open wide?
Identify this place and get up from your rut.
And stop allowing the devil to keep kicking your butt!

Love

Love is real character built from inside.

Deep down in your heart is where I abide.

Love is the power and ability

To know Me by My Spirit and see reality.

Love is the ability to look up above,

To love one another in spite of.

Love forgets the old and sees the new.

Love sees the future inside of you.

Love makes room for one to grow.

There is no perfect person. Look at you;

I'm sure you know.

Love isn't smiling and grinning in my face,

When you can't stand the sight of me,
which is really the case.

Love doesn't have an attitude and
hopes to still be blessed.

You can't say that you love me and not be put to test.

Love doesn't accuse and sow discord.

KIM K. SANDERS

Stop that gossip. Shut that mouth.
That's something you can't afford.
Love is not pretending to be what you're not
When all you have to do is use what you got.
Love doesn't judge, because you really can't see
All that God is doing on the inside of me.
Love is not carnal, but sees spiritually.
It doesn't ask why and loves unconditionally.
Love doesn't wonder, "Why have
I been misunderstood?"
Love has nothing to prove, even if you wish you could.
Love because you know it's just the right thing to do,
Not based on others and how they're treating you.
Love will set you free if you're real with yourself.
Love is the answer to healing and good health.
Love produces power; now you've got the key
To the unhidden treasure to keep the victory.
Now that you know it's love that you've
been searching for,
Tell the devil he must go. Now you must shut the door.

Sight Without Vision

You have sight but no vision; now, how can that be?

Carnal, carnal, carnal is your reality.

Eyes have not seen what God has prepared.

But you can't receive those things being religious and scared

Open up your heart and let the Word come in.

Renew your mind to vision and walk away from sin.

Change your way of thinking so you can believe

For all the hidden treasures, God wants you to receive.

All that God requires is faith like a mustard seed.

You must sow it and grow it before

He can meet the need.

The natural man can't receive; it's foolishness to him.

The things that God is speaking, they come from the Spirit Realm.

"Ha, Ha, this is crazy, I can't see!" says the carnal mind.

Look for Me says God; seek and ye shall find!

The Spirit Of Average

Break the spirit of average by taking off every limit.

Going after your destiny, not being fearful, complacent or timid.

It's been a long journey and the time has finally come

For those who are not closed-minded, playing crazy and stuck in dumb.

Average is a spirit keeping you on lock down,

With a messed up mentality when opportunities come around.

Excuses you make, afraid to step out,

Thinking you have faith when you're really full of doubt.

Faith is the substance of things you can't see,

Making ideas, dreams and desires become reality.

Average people sit and watch others create.

They're full of talk, envy, fear, jealousy and hate.

HUSHHHH GOD IS TALKING

Wanting the success of others but not
willing to pay the price,

Gambling with the odds, forever rolling dice.

Dice represents the game that you continue to play

While life, vision, hope and your future fade away.

"Mirror, mirror on the wall," who am I talking to?

The average person who's still broke;
am I talking to you?

Why Are You Broke?

Why are you broke? It's a question we should all ask.

Let's deal with the truth of the matter;
let's all take off the mask.

The reason that you're broke is a result of bad seeds,

Not knowing how to manage money,
or perhaps planting among weeds.

It could be that you're not a tither,
which affects how you receive,

A principle and a law that works,
regardless of how you believe.

It's a principle that works every time.

All God requires out of a dollar is a dime.

There's no seed sown that hasn't given birth.

Whether good or bad, every seed has its worth.

There's a price to pay when you don't know.

The laws of prosperity in your life it will show.

Maybe you're trying to live above your means,

HUSHHHH GOD IS TALKING

Trying to keep up with the Joneses,
buying extravagant things.

Now, who are the Joneses anyway,

Who're keeping you in bondage and causing you delay?

This is one of the reasons people get into debt,

Not trusting in God to keep their needs met.

Then there's the credit card game that people play,

Caught up in the system of the world every day.

Then there're you that are passive and have no drive

To go after your money to bring vision alive.

Are you weak minded, lazy, or afraid to step out?

Determination, faith and desire will
bring your money about.

What will it take to come out of this whirlwind?

The kingdom of God's system is the
only way to depend.

You must catch hold of the principle of giving;

It's the key that unlocks prosperity living.

If you're tired of being broke,
there's no one else to blame.

Make the decision that you're coming out,
and don't get back in the game.

Are You Ready To Get Married?

Are you ready to get married? Are you ready to commit?

Marriage is not like dating. One minute you're in; next minute you quit.

Let's take a moment and reflect on what marriage really means.

I'd like to uncover some of the hidden things.

When things get rough and times get tough,

Will you still have a fight in you to make it through the stuff?

Will you be able to say till death do us part?

Will you be ready to walk out if things get hard?

Will you be able to stay in sickness and in health?

Or is your only concern the riches and the wealth?

Ask yourself these questions:

Is this love that I feel?

Are you truly the one for me? Is this God's perfect will?

HUSHHHH GOD IS TALKING

Am I caught up in the glamour of getting married?
Am I looking for a hook-up? Am I looking to be carried?
Will I want to back out when things don't go my way?
Am I willing to submit to my mate every day?
What do I have to give and what will they have to add?
Will I have a life of happiness or will I always be sad?

Will there always be drama because
we're not on the same level?

Believe me, if you don't know,
you'll have problems with the devil.

Can I really be myself? Will you try to change me?

Are your insecurities a hindrance?

Will you always let them be?

Do you think you'll be treated like a king or a queen?

Or will the person that you marry be foul,
irritable, and mean?

Will undiscussed issues come up from the past?

Will it affect your future, an effect that will last?

What types of generational curses are in their family?

What strongholds am I dealing with?

Do you want to be free?

KIM K. SANDERS

Am I really equipped to deal with this type of thing?

There's more to marriage than the
wedding dress and ring.

Then there's sex. Who will be satisfied?

Your body won't be your own. Will someone be denied?

Will there be kids involved? How will they be raised?

What will you be teaching them and
can they follow your ways?

Do you argue all the time, fuss and fight?

Think twice if you think marriage
will change this overnight.

Well what about money? Know the
situation ahead of time.

Can you really say, "All I have is yours
and all you have is mine?"

This is a lot to digest, a lot to think about.

If you don't know the answers,
then that's a sign of doubt.

I'm not trying to scare you, I'm just provoking you to see

The truth people don't think about that's a reality.

Now think about this. Don't be in denial,
don't pretend, be real.

Consider all that's been said before you sign the deal.

Is He Ready To Be A Pastor?

Can he handle his finances in the home?

If not, he won't be able to handle finances in the dome.

Does he have wisdom to handle situations
that will arise?

When faced with major decisions, will he compromise?

Can he stand the pressure, criticism and persecution?

Or, will he get offended with the
people and allow confusion?

Does he love people? How does he interact with others?

Does he have a servant's heart or one that covers?

Is he sensitive to his own family's needs?

Or, does he go around to others doing good deeds?

What about integrity? Is he a man that God can trust?

Can he keep his word as a pastor?

These things are a must.

Is the Word of God working in his life?

KIM K. SANDERS

How can he teach faith if he's full of strife?

Is he obedient and submissive to God's authority?

If not, he'll draw rebellious people and his
children will be unruly.

Does his wife respect and submit to him?

Or, does she run around talking about him to

Pookie and them?

Is his home in order? Is there family unity?

Does he have patience and stability?

Has he been prepared and proven through
teaching and by example?

Is he running around chasing women,
desiring to taste and sample?

Does he know the heart of God?

Can he carry out God's vision?

Does he have his own agenda?

Does he understand his mission?

Is he totally sold out and has he counted up the cost?

There's a price to pay for the anointing
if you're going to be the boss.

Does he understand that it's not an option?

HUSHHHH GOD IS TALKING

he must pray and fast

In order to lead a flock, in order for him to last.

Some men are in love with the image of being a pastor,

But fail to realize it's a call, which is the
most important factor.

Do you think he's ready to be a pastor?

Who am I talking to?

Don't overlook the fact that I may be talking to you.

Why Do You Think The Way That You Do?

Why do you think the way that you do?

It's because you won't allow your mind to renew.

You have twisted thinking, and you can't really see

How things really are and how things can really be.

A false value system has been planted in your mind.

It started when you were young;
think back and let's rewind.

As a child there were things that you were taught.

Seeds planted in your conscious,

a seed that became a thought.

There are four different factors that
worked to shape your belief.

Things the enemy used to start this journey to your grief.

First is your social environment,

which affects the world around you.

HUSHHHH GOD IS TALKING

It imposes certain perceived truths about life and the
way you view.

Second, authority figures who teach us
certain things about living.

Those we were told to respect not even knowing what
they were giving.

Such as parents, relatives, friends and teachers
along with unlearned, carnal, raggedy life preachers

Thirdly, our minds have been shaped to accept
repetitious information.

What you believe can affect your decisions
and even your reputation.

As a man thinketh in his heart, the Word says, so is he.

That's why it's critical what you think;
it will affect who you can be.

Finally, your belief system is shaped and developed
by things you go through.

The most potent impact on your mind
designed to influence you.

Give yourself the opportunity for your
thoughts to be diverted.

One can tell by the way you talk that your
thinking has been perverted.

Let me use as an example things that you may say,

Words that you often use; I'll prove it if I may.

"I don't know how I'm going to make ends meet,"

As if you serve a God of defeat.

"I'd better not give all that money as a seed,"

As if God can't really meet your need.

"Well, if it's God's will, then He'll heal me,"

When Jesus paid the price for you at Calvary.

"I'm broke and I don't have any money,"

When the Promised Land is flowing with milk and honey.

"I'm living from check to check," is what you confess

When God is trying to show you that you are blessed.

"It just seems like things will never change;

I can't see my way out."

I guarantee you with thoughts like that,
you're a person full of doubt.

"I can never get ahead, I got too many bills,
and I'll always be in debt,"

It's a shame you've adopted this pattern of thinking

And, poisoning others I bet.

HUSHHHH GOD IS TALKING

Shall I go on? I think I made myself clear.

That you're living a life of torment and fear

"I don't think like that," you may be saying;
however, I'm still talking to you.

Now, let's be honest. Just ask yourself,

"What thoughts am I yielding to?"

It's obvious that you're dull of hearing
and haven't heard

What God is really saying according to His Word.

You may not say it out of your mouth,
but these things you believe.

They're silent thoughts of the enemy in
your mind that you've conceived.

You must admit that you've missed out

On opportunities that came your way.

Because you won't cast down imaginations,

You invite the enemy to come and play

The game is designed to keep your mind in bondage,

To keep you trapped in a prison cell,

To keep you deceived, whispering in
your ear that you will always fail.

KIM K. SANDERS

You'll never fulfill God's will for your life
if you don't change your thinking.

Being comfortable, content, and complacent

Will keep that strong hold stinking.

That demon will stay right where it is,
smelling just like defeat,

You continuing to be subject to him,
never being complete.

The devil will keep you right where he wants you,
continuing to operate.

Paralyzed, torment, held captive in your mind

Is it enough for you to hate?

I know that these are strong words,
but look at what the devil has done.

The sad part is that you really don't know
that the battle has just begun.

What Is Wrong With You, Man?

What is wrong with the men of our society today,
especially men of the Word?

Acting ignorant, not owning up to the
teaching that you have heard.

You play crazy, like you don't know what to do,

When there's opportunity everyday around you.

You let the devil come in and take
advantage of your household.

In your place, she stands because you
won't rise up and be bold.

She brings home the bacon, fries it up in several pans,

And you're still applying the pressure,
making all of your demands.

You want her to be the watchman, the warrior, your
freak and your "ho."

And that's not enough, because you still
want some more.

She washes your funky drawers and
takes good care of you,

KIM K. SANDERS

While none of her needs are being met,
and that ain't nothing new.

What's wrong with you, man?

Who do you expect her to be?

Your maid, your concubine, fulfilling your
every fantasy?

Now you tell me, man, "Do you think this is right?"

Expecting a stress-free marriage and
never expecting a fight?

Take responsibility and take your rightful place.

Get down on your knees and get down on your face.

Release her from your duties so she can fulfill her own.

Be the priest, the prophet and the king of your home.

Do the right thing and I guarantee
she'll rock your world.

Treat her like your queen and she'll be your fantasy girl.

CHAPTER FOUR

Prophetic Instructions

The Word

You have My promises and you have My Word.

Faith comes by hearing. Now say what you've heard!

All things are possible to them that believe;

You've got to see it in the Spirit so you can receive.

Angels are waiting; they'll hearken to your voice.

Only if you speak My Word, but it must be your choice.

The Word of God is true, and it cannot lie.

The Word of God is quick and alive with
power that you can't deny.

The Word of God is powerful and sharper
than any two-edged sword.

Every knee shall bow and every tongue shall confess

That Jesus Christ is Lord.

The Word of God will heal you and the

Word will set you free.

God's waiting on you to apply it,
so you can have victory.

HUSHHHH GOD IS TALKING

Stop sitting around being lazy and put the

Word of God in your mouth!

Stop meditating on the negative, which brings fear, unbelief and doubt.

You know that God is faithful and you know what you have to do.

Faith without work is dead, now the rest is up to you!

Keep It Moving

You gotta keep it moving; stop living in the past.

All the hurts, disappointments,
those relationships that didn't last.

It's time to move forward and see what's next,

And be free from the mental torment
causing you to be perplexed.

So what? It didn't happen the way you thought it should,

And it didn't go down the way you thought it would.

It doesn't mean that you're a failure;
so let go of the regret,

Holding yourself in bondage to a non existing debt.

For those of you who feel like your life has
been full of mistakes,

I see your fears, all the tears and how your heart aches.

You've had spiritual miscarriages, major
setbacks to cause your delay.

HUSHHHH GOD IS TALKING

But I declare to you from this very moment,

"This is the beginning of a new day!"

No more sabotages, spiritual abortions, harassments.

Nothing else to set you back.

You must overthrow every diabolical assignment

And come against every devilish counter attack.

Bind every hindrance, every distraction
and every evil spirit;

Speak these words to the heavenlies

And decree that satan hears and fears it.

Angels are hearkening to the voice of God's

Word as I speak.

"I command every principality and every
power to fall weak.

I have authority over you satan and

I break every power

Off the people under the sound of my
voice in this very hour.

I break every curse, and I command every
man and woman to be free!

I command your immediate release,

KIM K. SANDERS

Spirit, soul and body, to divine liberty!

All demonic defilement, attachments and satanic plantings I uproot!

I decree and declare that I will begin to manifest and produce fruit!

The yoke of bondage from my past is now permanently eradicated!

The satanic residue and all effect have been barricaded!

I target, and I annihilate the hidden agenda of the enemy,

And I uncover every operation and every strategy!

My prayers are like arrows;

I hit bulls eyes in the realm of the spirit when I pray;

I come against every demonic force that stands in the way!

I hit every fiery dart, every tactic, and every scheme and demolish every plan.

I cancel, abort, nullify and dismantle all plots

Against every woman, child and man.

As I stand in my mantle clothed in the authority of God,

Having the breastplate of righteousness on with my feet shod,

HUSHHHH GOD IS TALKING

I shine the light of God's Word on every dark place.

I plead the blood of Jesus over every situation and over every case.

I close satan's access to my mind

And demolish the high places erected in my soul.

I decree and declare in my life that satan has no more control!"

Seal this prayer with the Word, the blood of

Jesus and the name.

Now don't look back; keep it moving 'cause your life won't be the same!

For Such A Time As This

God has graced you for such a time as this,

And the devil must return back to the abyss.

The devil ain't nothin' but a defeated foe;

The battle is the Lord's, God wants you to know.

Put on your dancin' shoes and let the praise begin

Because all you've gone through has come to an end.

Hallelujah to the King for all that He has done!

You ain't seen nothing yet; life has just begun!

So, get your house in order and do what you know to do;

There's no time to waste, blessings are waiting for you!

God wants to use you; so, prepare yourself before Him.

You don't have time to worry and be concerned about Pookie and them.

HUSHHHH GOD IS TALKING

So, get before His presence and do what you do best.

Where there's peace, joy and wisdom, enter into His rest.

God desires that you walk in your call

God desires that you walk in His all!

It's Time To Fly

Spread your wings like an eagle; it's time to fly.

Stop sitting around wondering when, how, and why.

Rise up and fly as high as you can.

Take your rightful position; it's time for you to stand.

You've crawled, you've walked; you've even tried to run.

Don't even think about getting tired cause the race has just begun.

You'll fly here, you'll fly there; you'll fly everywhere.

You'll fly as far as you can see; with this flight there's no airfare.

You've asked Me to enlarge your territory, so stretch out your wings.

You must be willing to go the distance to get the hidden things.

Fly baby fly, fly as high as you can see.

The sky's the limit to all that you can be!

From Caterpillar To Butterfly

From caterpillar to butterfly, it's your time to come out.

It's time to come out of hiding and show what you're all about.

Loose your fears, loose your concerns and be who you really are.

No more excuses because the caps been taken off the jar.

It's up to you to fly, you've already been transformed.

You can't go back to the old because it's no longer the norm.

Transferred from a caterpillar to a butterfly;

It's the real you. Now tell the old you goodbye.

You've shed off some things and broke into the light.

You've entered into the daybreak, while yet it was night.

Fly in the direction that God has for you.

Don't be afraid to fly into doors that are new.

I'm taking you places but you can't be afraid

KIM K. SANDERS

To release the butterfly in you that only I made.

It's time to come forth; it's your time to shine.

I desire to favor and feature what's mine.

Look For The New

You're entering into a season of new.

New opportunities and new favor await you.

From this day forward, focus only on
things that are necessary.

All things that are dead, I command you to bury.

There's been a shift in the Spirit and in this Nation,

As the world cries out in great anticipation.

It's time to pray Saints, like never before,

For all the things that God has in store.

Pray for this country, for our nation,
pray and take a stand.

Pray that God will release to our president

His Master plan.

It's time for the church to rise up and take her place,

The place of travail where we lay on our face.

God needs a legal right to intervene in the Earth,

KIM K. SANDERS

To produce the new, but you must pray and give birth.
Give birth to the new that you desire to see,
In this nation, your personal life and in your family
What is the purpose and what is the reason?
So God can transition you into this new season!

It's Time To Give

It's time to give like never before

For God's hidden treasures that He has in store.

Treasures of darkness, hidden riches of the secret place

Only for those who will seek God's face.

This is not the time to hold back what's in your hand;

It's time to apply pressure with your seed and demand.

We're in the hour of manifestation,
but the violent must take it by force.

You can't afford to be distracted; you must be
focused and stay on course.

Distractions will try to come in various
types and different forms.

Recognize them when they come
because it won't come in the norm.

It's very important and crucial that
you hear where to sow,

KIM K. SANDERS

For that uncommon seed to multiply and grow.

When God begins to speak, immediately
respond and obey.

Don't miss the opportunity;
it will cause you much delay.

Take heed to this Word; this is the time to give.

You can't depend on the world's
system if you really desire to live

There will be seedtime and harvest as long
as the earth remains.

Warning comes before destruction;
things are about to change.

If you have seed in the ground, it will be for your good.

If you wait for the famine to come, you'll be
wishing that you could.

So don't get caught eating up your seed

For something the devil will try to make
you think you need.

You'll be challenged in your giving to
come out your comfort zone.

It will separate the sons and daughters
from those who will walk alone.

HUSHHHH GOD IS TALKING

God is speeding up the process;

He's redeeming the time for you.

He's requiring much of your seed, for doors you're about to go through!

Don't Be Distracted

Don't be distracted by things around;

Distractions are designed to make you lose ground.

Know how to recognize it when it shows up;

It comes in various forms and disguises,
sneaky and abrupt.

This is not the time to get side-tracked

With things of no substance to set your life back.

The devil will use people and bring them on the scene

All of a sudden out of nowhere,
so be discernful and be keen.

He wants to draw your attention and lead you astray

When destiny is calling so don't be
drawn and pulled away.

He'll check out your patterns and use it as bait;

He'll create situations to keep you unable to
concentrate.

HUSHHHH GOD IS TALKING

It's very important to be sober and keep
your mind clear,

Not get out of position and stay focused
so you can hear.

Keep your eyes on the vision that God has given you.

This is the year of release and it's
about to come through.

You must cut off all figs from your tree;

Curse it at the root, let it die and let it be.

No more distractions by things around;

You will see it when it comes, let it fall to the ground.

It's Time To Get Your Money

It's time to get your money, stop sitting around.

Your money is hidden for you, waiting to be found.

Provision is looking for the vision;
it ain't looking for you.

It won't show up for nothing; it has to
have something to pursue.

Your faith must match your assignment;
you've got to come through Me

For this wealth transferring anointing,
power and ability.

The enemy's had you on a goose chase,
stuck in the outer court,

Attaching you to the world's system, making you
believe its report.

You've got to go to the third realm,
where I will give you a plan.

That's the place where I speak, only to your spirit man.

HUSHHHH GOD IS TALKING

You don't have moments to waste;
you're making up for lost time.

Take all that's been stolen from you,
make satan pay back every dime!

Your quality of life will determine
what you do every day.

You need wisdom for the assignment,
for success to come your way

Wisdom opens your eyes to an opportunity.

You'll be able to spot things that others don't see.

Stop making excuses, blaming Me
for your lack of success.

Saying you're waiting on Me to move,
sitting in the comfort of your flesh.

It's time to be productive and use what's in your hand

To produce the type of harvest your vision will demand.

Remove the mental barriers that are blocking your path.

It's time to get your money; now you go do the math!

Go Get Your Money Now!

Go get your money now; the violent taketh by force!

The vision is waiting so you can finish your course.

What are you waiting for?

You've already got the plan.

Certainly you're not waiting on Me and
certainly you're not waiting on man.

You make your way prosperous and cause good success.

The wealth of the wicked is laid up for the just;

So don't accept anything less.

You've got gifts, you've got talents and creative ability.

You've got wisdom, knowledge and
resources to make vision a reality.

What do you have in your hands to turn into a seed?

You sow it, I'll grow it and you'll have what you need.

You can't neglect spiritual laws and think
money will fall out of the sky.

HUSHHHH GOD IS TALKING

Spiritual laws and natural laws, both, you must apply!

The anointing has been released to bring
your money to pass,

A continuous flow of revenues, money that will last.

Remember the Lord your God who
gives you the power to get wealth.

Remember it's all about vision; the
provision is not for self!

Get Ready For Your Husband

Start praying for your husband to come on the scene;
Ask God to show him his Queen.
He who finds a wife finds a good thing;
So, put on your pearls and show forth your bling.
Stop walking around looking raggedy, old and crazy;
Fix up yourself, stop lying around being lazy.
What is it that you think a man is looking for?
It's not just breast, legs and hips but so much more.
I'm just saying, all that stuff plays a small part,
But it's not the thing that will capture his heart.
Not saying you shouldn't know how to work your stuff,
But, at this point you should not still be a diamond in the rough.

If you're ready for your husband,
you should already be perfected

HUSHHHH GOD IS TALKING

Because you don't want to be served on a
platter and be rejected.

I'm not implying that you're perfect
and don't have issues,

But preparation just eliminates unnecessary tissues.

The tissues of pain, crying, fighting and drama

You know, where you always have to keep
calling home to your mama.

So, ladies let's talk about what you need to do

To get yourself ready and prepared for your Boo.

First of all, let's go in the closet and get
rid of some bags,

So you won't send him on top of the roof;
the Bible calls it "nags."

Get rid of old thoughts of who used to rock your world,

Who did it like this and who made your toes curl.

Bae is gone girl and he ain't coming back.

So, we take authority over every mental attack.

You must cast down every imagination
that makes you meditate;

I curse every foul spirit that makes you masturbate.

So throw away the photos, the gifts and the toys,

Get rid of anything that brings wicked types of joys.

I break every soul-tie that's keeping you bound,

And, I command every stronghold in
your mind to be pulled down.

Next, allow emotional healing to take place.

So loving God and yourself can fill up your space.

Let pride, selfishness and haughtiness have an abortion

So humility, love and wisdom can be your portion.

Now, prayer and praise should be your new clothes,

So when the king sees the queen,
he'll say, "There she goes!"

Don't Try To Explain

Don't try to explain why you do the things you do.

Submit yourself to Me; I'm the One that you answer to.

People won't understand; so, don't try to explain

Things you do, things you say, how you think,
which seems insane.

I've taken you to another level,

a place most people aren't willing to go.

There's a price to pay to be here,
you've paid it and many don't know.

Many sacrifices have been made,
persecution on your behalf,

Those you've separated yourself from,
behind your back they laugh.

God shall not be mocked, but they
shall reap what they sow.

There are those that are reaping now
and it's sad that they don't even know.

KIM K. SANDERS

There are particular people that I told you not to trust.

Just as sure as I have shown you others,
see these as a must.

They are not really for you; though they smile; you
know that it's a lie.

Don't give place to the devil,
wasting time, wondering why.

I've called you to set a standard;

That's why I've pulled you away from the pack.

Take heed to the one's I've removed you from;

I forbid you to ever go back.

It's like a person that's been delivered
and set free from drugs.

If they ever go back for a hit, you know
the rest and what it does.

People may look at you and think
that you're being mean and rude.

Don't try to explain, you owe no explanation;
it will only cause a feud.

There's a certain level of maturity it takes to understand

The life that I've called you to,

not understood by the carnal man

HUSHHHH GOD IS TALKING

There will be those in your life that will
come and try to stay,

But this next mantle I'm placing on you,
may drive them completely away.

In order for them to last, they must be totally sold out.

They must reverence and understand
what your life is all about.

Some will look at you and say to themselves,

"Who does she/he think she/he is?"

But you'll discern and say to them,

"It's not my doing, it's all of His."

Touch not My anointed and do My prophets no harm.

Those who put their mouths on you,

I won't hesitate to stretch out My arm.

So don't compromise My child and don't try to explain.

Your reward for your obedience will be
more than you can contain!

He's A Good Man

He's a good man even though he doesn't
do everything right.

Stop expecting all things to be changed overnight.

Nobody's perfect and he will never be.

Pray that he strives to be like Me.

Those things in his life I will perfect.

There are things in your heart I will resurrect.

The passion and the romance I will restore;

The love will increase and you'll desire more.

Don't be afraid to open up your heart;

Put your trust in Me and let Me do My part.

All you have to do is totally yield;

I'll break down the wall and remove the shield.

The enemy's tried hard to make you cold blooded,

But My overwhelming love will
keep your heart flooded,

HUSHHHH GOD IS TALKING

Like a blood transfusion running through your veins
Washing away memories of every hurt and all pains.
Your cup will run over; it will overflow.
With the rivers of love in your life, it will show.
Your bowels of compassion will open up wide
As I cleanse and remove things on your inside.
He's a good man; so begin to anticipate
The changes, the promises. I won't hesitate!

A Couple To Be Admired

You're a couple to be admired; people are watching you.

God is using you as His example,
even as you sit in the pew.

Don't think it's strange that it's been your desire

To have a marriage full of romance, passion and fire.

It's how I designed it and called it to be;

I've chosen you My son and daughter to represent Me.

You've been through many things,
but it's a part of the call.

I've allowed you to come through so you
can minister to all.

There's a unique anointing that I've placed on your life,

Never to be compared to any husband or wife.

Be confident in yourselves and represent Me well;

Many doors will open and your testimony you will tell.

You will be strength to those who are
watching from afar;

HUSHHHH GOD IS TALKING

You may never see them, but know that they're
watching, yes they are!

Stay on your knees and don't let the devil come in;

You'll draw your strength from Me and
every time you'll win!

I say to you this day, you're a couple to be admired,

A God-ordained marriage made to be inspired!

THE END
Heaven Is A Real Place And So Is Hell

Heaven is a real place and so is hell.

Once you leave this Earth realm, you will be able to tell.

Don't deceive yourself in thinking that it's not real;

It's a place of reality, it's a place of your will.

You must turn to Jesus before it's too late;

It's not up for discussion and it's not up for debate.

It's not about your works and all of your good deeds;

It's about the blood of Jesus that
was shed to meet your needs.

He died on the cross so that you can live

A life of peace, joy, and love only He can give.

Some people might think that it's hell here on Earth,

But, nothing can compare to hell on the devil's turf.

You don't want to end up in the place

called the lake of fire;

HUSHHHH GOD IS TALKING

I refuse to believe and think that this is your real desire.

Jesus will be back soon; no man knows the hour;

He'll come like a thief in the night full of
glory and full of power!

There's a serious price to pay to live a life of sin;

It leads to a road of destruction that
comes to a dead end.

What profits a man to gain the whole
world and still lose his soul?

I beg of you, don't believe the lies and
stay under the devil's control.

ABOUT THE AUTHOR

As an authorized spokesman for God, Prophetess Kim K. Sanders speaks the prophetic utterances and heart of God. Boldly proclaiming God's message, she speaks of current issues, bringing warning, instructions and reproof, giving insight and foresight revealing the plans and will of God. Prophetess Kim is a Licensed Ordained Minister, an Anointed Minstrel, Psalmist, Prophetic Spoken Word Poet, and Published Author. Prophetess Kim is the Founder and President of Kim K. Sanders Ministries, Inc.

The Arkansas native has an extensive school of the arts background, which includes music, dance and drama. Kim's study of dance began at the age of nine with the late Dot Callanen, where she studied ballet, tap, and jazz. She became a company member and performed in several productions. Thereafter, Kim furthered her ballet studies with Antonio Mesa from France and the late Manolo Agullo, at the Arkansas Arts Center. She traveled and appeared in various productions such as "The Red Shoes," "Peter and the Wolf" and many others. Kim later made her debut as a Professional Ballet Dancer in the Senior Company of Ballet Arkansas under the direction of the late Lorraine Cranford. She performed in "The Nutcracker Suite," "Swan Lake" and "Giselle." She also made several solo guest appearances.

Kim's study of Music began at an early age and continued as a Music Major at Cameron University in Lawton Oklahoma. All her life she had a burning passion and deep desire to sing, dance, act and play music. Little did she know that God was preparing her all along as a vessel to carry His glory. Kim's gifts are used to set the atmosphere for the Holy Spirit, and to accompany her for the preaching of the Word. As Prophetess Kim sings and plays prophetic sounds from heaven, the Mantle of David rests on her to cast out demons. People are brought into the very presence of God, receiving peace, joy and all manner of healings and deliverances as the power of music penetrates the atmosphere and pierces the forces of darkness with the fire of God!

Prophetess Kim has a unique deliverance ministry in which she ministers life to those who are spiritually dead, healing to the broken-hearted, and deliverance to those held captive living in bondage to the god of this world. God has given Kim a spirit led boldness to minister truth with confidence, love, and the authority that will penetrate directly to the spirit of man, challenging men and women to repentance, obedience, and a life of complete wholeness. As a "Spiritual Bulldozer" in the Kingdom of God, Prophetess Kim is continuously disrupting, penetrating and tearing down the powers of darkness, digging deep, uprooting everything that's not of God. Kim is the proud wife of former Circuit Judge Ernest Sanders Jr. and the devoted mother of two children, Trinity Latrice Eubanks and Ernest Sanders III.

Kim is the author of the best selling book, *"Loose Your Money."* For more information about online classes, live events and booking Kim, visit **www.kimksanders.com.**

KIM K. SANDERS

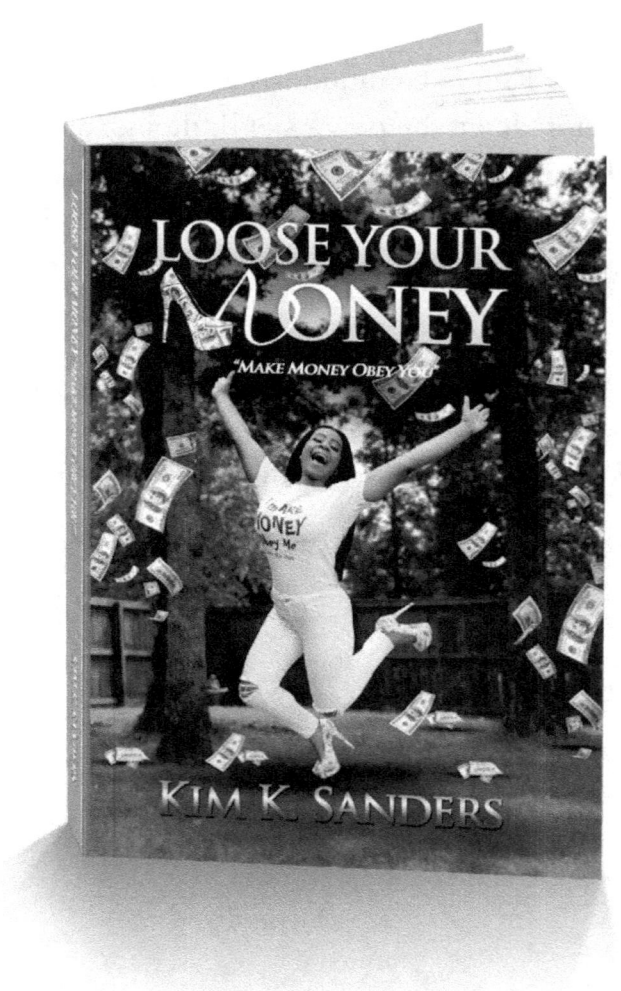

HUSHHHH GOD IS TALKING

"Loose Your Money" is for the person who's ready to stop chasing money and start attracting extraordinary wealth daily. In this book, Kim K. Sanders reveals hidden truths and shares divine revelation that will properly position you to receive prosperity. This powerful book is packed with valuable content and applicable knowledge that will increase your mental capacity to build wealth.

ISBN: 978-0-9966222-0-2

GET YOUR COPY AT WWW.KIMKSANDERS.COM, AMAZON OR BARNES & NOBLES.

www.ingramcontent.com/pod-product-compliance
Lightning Source LLC
Chambersburg PA
CBHW070626300426
44113CB00010B/1670